The Art of Fearless Speaking: Embrace Confidence on Any

Miller James

Copyright © [2023]

Title: The Art of Fearless Speaking: Embrace Confidence on Any
Author's: Miller James

All rights reserved. No part of this publication may be reproduced, stored in a retrieval system, or transmitted in any form or by any means, electronic, mechanical, photocopying, recording, or otherwise, without the prior written permission of the publisher or author, except in the case of brief quotations embodied in critical reviews and certain other non-commercial uses permitted by copyright law.

This book was printed and published by [Publisher's: **Miller James**] in [2023]

ISBN:

TABLE OF CONTENT

Chapter 1: The Power of Fearless Speaking   07

Understanding the Impact of Fear on Public Speaking Confidence

Identifying Common Fears and Anxieties in Public Speaking

Chapter 2: Unleashing Your Inner Confidence   11

Embracing Your Unique Voice and Style

Cultivating Self-Awareness and Authenticity on Stage

Harnessing the Power of Positive Thinking

Chapter 3: Overcoming Fear through Preparation   17

Developing an Effective Speech Outline

Researching and Gathering Supporting Materials

Practicing Techniques for Memorization and Delivery

Chapter 4: Mastering Non-Verbal Communication   23

Understanding the Impact of Body Language on Audience Perception

Enhancing Gestures, Posture, and Eye Contact

Utilizing Vocal Variety and Tone to Convey Confidence

Chapter 5: Connecting with Your Audience   29

Establishing Rapport and Engaging the Crowd

Utilizing Storytelling Techniques to Captivate and Inspire

Handling Questions and Feedback with Confidence

Chapter 6: Managing Nerves and Handling Unexpected Challenges   35

Implementing Relaxation Techniques to Calm Pre-Speech Anxiety

Dealing with Technical Difficulties and Unexpected Interruptions

Turning Mistakes into Opportunities for Growth

Chapter 7: Enhancing Your Presentation Skills   42

Utilizing Visual Aids Effectively to Enhance Communication

Incorporating Humor and Engaging Techniques to Connect with the Audience

Creating Memorable Endings and Calls to Action

Chapter 8: Embracing Feedback and Continuous Improvement   48

Seeking Constructive Criticism to Enhance Performance

Developing a Personalized Feedback and Improvement Plan

Embracing a Growth Mindset for Ongoing Success

Chapter 9: Overcoming Fear of Specific Speaking Situations   54

Speaking in Small Group Settings or Meetings

Presenting to Large Audiences or Conferences

Overcoming Fear of Public Speaking Online or through Video Conferencing

Chapter 10: Maintaining Fearless Speaking in Everyday Life   60

Applying Public Speaking Techniques in Professional Settings

Utilizing Fearless Speaking Skills in Personal Relationships and Social Settings

Embracing Fearless Communication in Advocacy and Leadership Roles

Conclusion: Embrace Confidence on Any Stage   66

Chapter 1: The Power of Fearless Speaking

Understanding the Impact of Fear on Public Speaking Confidence

Fear is a powerful emotion that can have a significant impact on our lives. It can hold us back from pursuing our dreams, hinder our ability to communicate effectively, and diminish our self-confidence. When it comes to public speaking, fear plays a particularly influential role in determining our level of confidence on stage.

Public speaking is a common fear shared by many individuals, regardless of their background or profession. The mere thought of standing in front of an audience can trigger feelings of anxiety, self-doubt, and fear of judgment. These emotions can manifest in physical symptoms such as sweaty palms, a racing heart, or even a shaky voice.

Understanding the impact of fear on public speaking confidence is crucial for anyone seeking to conquer this fear and develop their self-confidence. By recognizing the underlying causes of this fear, we can begin to address them head-on and build the necessary skills to become fearless speakers.

One of the primary reasons fear affects public speaking confidence is the fear of failure or making mistakes. We worry about stumbling over our words, forgetting what we wanted to say, or facing difficult questions from the audience. This fear of failure can create a vicious cycle, where our anxiety increases, leading to a further decline in confidence.

Another factor that contributes to fear is the fear of judgment or criticism. We worry about what others will think of us, whether they will find our ideas interesting or valuable. This fear of judgment can cause us to doubt our abilities and undermine our self-confidence.

To overcome these fears and boost public speaking confidence, it is essential to adopt a growth mindset. Instead of viewing public speaking as a test of our abilities, we should see it as an opportunity for growth and learning. By reframing our mindset, we can approach each speaking engagement with curiosity and a willingness to improve.

Additionally, preparation and practice are key to building confidence. By thoroughly preparing our content and rehearsing our delivery, we can reduce anxiety and increase our sense of control. The more we practice, the more comfortable and confident we become in our ability to deliver a compelling presentation.

In conclusion, fear plays a significant role in shaping our public speaking confidence. However, by understanding the impact of fear and taking proactive steps to address it, we can become fearless speakers. By adopting a growth mindset, preparing thoroughly, and practicing regularly, we can overcome our fears and embrace confidence on any stage. Remember, everyone can develop self-confidence in public speaking with the right strategies and mindset.

Identifying Common Fears and Anxieties in Public Speaking

For many people, the thought of speaking in public can be a daunting and anxiety-inducing experience. Whether you are addressing a small group of colleagues or delivering a presentation to a large audience, the fear of public speaking is a common and natural response. In this subchapter, we will explore some of the most common fears and anxieties associated with public speaking and provide insights to help you overcome them, so you can embrace confidence on any stage.

One of the most prevalent fears in public speaking is the fear of judgment. Many individuals worry about being scrutinized by their audience, fearing that they will be perceived as incompetent or uninteresting. This fear is often rooted in a lack of self-confidence and a fear of failure. By recognizing that everyone has their own insecurities and that the audience is usually more supportive than critical, you can begin to shift your mindset and embrace self-assurance.

Another common anxiety is the fear of forgetting your lines or losing track of your thoughts. This fear often stems from a lack of preparation or unfamiliarity with the topic. The key to overcoming this fear is thorough preparation and practice. By knowing your material inside and out, you can build a foundation of confidence that will help you stay focused and composed even if you stumble over your words.

The fear of public speaking also includes physical manifestations such as trembling hands, a racing heart, or a dry mouth. These physical symptoms are caused by the body's natural stress response, commonly known as the fight-or-flight response. Understanding that these symptoms are a normal reaction to stress can help you accept them and manage them more effectively. Techniques such as deep breathing exercises, visualization, and positive self-talk can help calm your nerves and regain control of your body's response.

Furthermore, the fear of public speaking often stems from a fear of the unknown. The fear of what could go wrong – technical difficulties, unexpected questions, or interruptions – can be paralyzing. By practicing and familiarizing yourself with potential challenges, you can anticipate and prepare for them, reducing the element of surprise and boosting your confidence.

In conclusion, identifying and acknowledging common fears and anxieties in public speaking is the first step towards conquering them. By understanding that these fears are shared by many and can be overcome, you can begin to develop the self-confidence necessary to become a fearless speaker. With practice, preparation, and a positive mindset, you can embrace confidence on any stage and become an effective and engaging public speaker. Remember, everyone starts somewhere, and the journey towards fearlessness begins with taking the first step.

Chapter 2: Unleashing Your Inner Confidence

Embracing Your Unique Voice and Style

In the journey towards becoming a fearless speaker, one of the most crucial steps is embracing your unique voice and style. Each one of us possesses a distinct perspective, personality, and way of expressing ourselves. It is this uniqueness that makes our message not only powerful but also relatable to others. When we embrace our individuality, we unlock our true potential and find the confidence to speak fearlessly.

Self-confidence plays a significant role in the development of our voice and style. It is the belief in our own abilities and worth that allows us to step onto any stage with conviction. However, building self-confidence is not an overnight process; it requires patience, practice, and self-reflection.

To embrace your unique voice and style, start by exploring your passions and interests. What topics ignite a fire within you? What makes you come alive when you speak about it? By identifying these areas, you can align your speaking engagements with your genuine interests, allowing your true voice to shine through.

Next, embrace vulnerability. It can be intimidating to share our authentic selves with the world, fearing judgment or rejection. But it is through vulnerability that we connect with others on a deeper level. Share personal stories, experiences, and lessons learned. By opening up, you not only become more relatable but also inspire others to do the same.

Another essential aspect of embracing your unique voice and style is understanding your audience. Each individual has their own set of beliefs, values, and experiences. Tailoring your message to resonate with your specific audience ensures that your voice is heard and understood. Research your audience beforehand, understand their needs and concerns, and speak to them in a language they can relate to.

Lastly, practice, practice, practice! The more you speak, the more comfortable you become with your own voice and style. Take every opportunity to speak in front of others, whether it's at a small gathering or a larger event. Each experience will help refine your delivery, allowing you to embrace your unique qualities as a speaker.

Remember, embracing your unique voice and style is a continuous process. As you grow and evolve, so will your speaking abilities. Have faith in yourself and your message, and let your true voice shine through. The world is waiting to hear what you have to say.

Cultivating Self-Awareness and Authenticity on Stage

In the world of public speaking, there is one undeniable truth: authenticity is the key to success. When you step onto a stage, whether it's a small gathering or a large conference, the audience can sense when you are being genuine and when you are not. In order to truly connect with your audience and deliver a powerful message, you must cultivate self-awareness and authenticity.

Self-awareness is the foundation of confidence. It is the ability to recognize and understand your own thoughts, emotions, and behaviors. By developing a deep understanding of yourself, you can harness your strengths and work on areas that may need improvement. When you are self-aware, you are able to project a sense of calm and authenticity on stage, which instantly captivates your audience.

To cultivate self-awareness, take the time to reflect on your experiences and identify your core values. What do you stand for? What message do you want to share with the world? By aligning your actions with your values, you will naturally exude authenticity on stage. Additionally, practice mindfulness techniques such as deep breathing and meditation to stay present in the moment and fully engage with your audience.

Authenticity goes hand in hand with self-awareness. It is the ability to be true to yourself and express your thoughts and emotions genuinely. When you are authentic on stage, you create a genuine connection with your audience. People are drawn to authenticity because it allows them to see your vulnerability and relate to your experiences.

To cultivate authenticity, start by embracing your unique voice and perspective. Do not try to mimic others or hide behind a mask. Your audience wants to hear your story, your ideas, and your passion. Be open and honest about your journey and let your true self shine through.

Remember, self-confidence comes from within. It is not about being perfect or trying to please everyone. When you cultivate self-awareness and authenticity, you will naturally radiate confidence on stage. Embrace your unique qualities and trust in your ability to deliver a powerful message. Your audience will be inspired by your authenticity and will be more likely to connect with your message.

In conclusion, cultivating self-awareness and authenticity on stage is crucial for anyone looking to improve their self-confidence in public speaking. By being self-aware, you can harness your strengths and align your actions with your values. By being authentic, you create a genuine connection with your audience and inspire them with your unique voice. Embrace your fears, embrace your true self, and embrace confidence on any stage.

Harnessing the Power of Positive Thinking

In today's fast-paced world, self-confidence has become more crucial than ever. Whether you're speaking in front of a large audience, participating in a job interview, or simply navigating through your daily interactions, having a strong sense of self-confidence can make all the difference. However, building and maintaining self-confidence is not always an easy task. That's where the power of positive thinking comes into play.

Positive thinking is a mindset that focuses on the potential for success, growth, and happiness. It involves training your mind to see the positive aspects of any situation, even in the face of challenges or setbacks. By harnessing the power of positive thinking, you can develop a resilient and unwavering self-confidence that will empower you to tackle any stage with fearlessness.

One of the first steps in harnessing the power of positive thinking is to become aware of your thoughts and self-talk. Pay attention to the language you use when talking to yourself and challenge any negative or self-limiting beliefs. Replace them with positive affirmations and statements that reinforce your abilities and strengths. By consciously choosing positive thoughts, you can rewire your brain to focus on the possibilities rather than the limitations.

Another key aspect of positive thinking is to surround yourself with positivity. Seek out individuals who uplift and support you, and limit your exposure to negative influences. Whether it's through books, podcasts, or motivational speakers, immerse yourself in positive content that can inspire and motivate you on your journey towards self-confidence.

Additionally, practicing gratitude can be a powerful tool in harnessing the power of positive thinking. Take a few moments each day to reflect on the things you are grateful for. By shifting your focus to the blessings in your life, you cultivate a mindset of abundance and appreciation, further boosting your self-confidence.

Finally, remember to celebrate your successes, no matter how small they may seem. Recognize your achievements and give yourself credit for your hard work and progress. This positive reinforcement will not only increase your self-confidence but also serve as a reminder of your capabilities.

In conclusion, harnessing the power of positive thinking is a transformative practice that can enhance your self-confidence in any area of life. By adopting a positive mindset, surrounding yourself with positivity, practicing gratitude, and celebrating your successes, you can cultivate an unshakable sense of self-assurance. Embrace the power of positive thinking and unlock your fearless speaking potential on any stage.

Chapter 3: Overcoming Fear through Preparation

Developing an Effective Speech Outline

In the realm of public speaking, one of the most crucial steps in delivering a successful presentation is developing an effective speech outline. Whether you are a seasoned speaker or someone who struggles with self-confidence, having a well-structured outline can transform your speech and help you communicate your ideas with clarity and conviction. This subchapter aims to guide every individual, regardless of their level of confidence, in crafting a powerful speech outline that will leave a lasting impact on any audience.

The first step in developing an effective speech outline is to clearly define your objective. Ask yourself, what is the main message or purpose of your speech? Are you aiming to inform, persuade, or entertain your audience? Once you have a clear objective in mind, you can begin organizing your thoughts and ideas in a logical manner.

Next, it is important to identify the key points that support your main message. These points should be concise, relevant, and well-researched. Remember, your goal is to engage your audience, so make sure your key points are interesting and relatable. You can use personal anecdotes, statistics, or quotes to support your arguments and add credibility to your speech.

Once you have identified your key points, it is time to consider the structure of your speech. A well-structured outline typically consists of an introduction, body, and conclusion. The introduction should grab the audience's attention, state your main message, and provide a brief overview of what will be discussed. The body of your speech should be divided into sections, each addressing a specific key point. Use transitions to smoothly guide your audience from one point to another. Finally, the conclusion should summarize your main points and leave the audience with a memorable takeaway.

In addition to structuring your speech, it is essential to consider your delivery style. Your outline should include cues for pauses, emphasis, and body language. These elements contribute to your overall confidence and presence on stage.

Remember, developing an effective speech outline is a process that requires practice and refinement. By investing time and effort into crafting a well-structured outline, you can overcome self-confidence issues and deliver a powerful speech that captivates your audience.

Researching and Gathering Supporting Materials

In the journey towards becoming a fearless speaker, one of the crucial steps is researching and gathering supporting materials. Your ability to present well-researched and credible information not only enhances your content but also boosts your self-confidence on stage. In this subchapter, we will delve into the art of researching and provide you with effective strategies to gather supporting materials for your speeches or presentations.

First and foremost, it is important to understand the significance of conducting thorough research. Researching allows you to gather facts, statistics, and examples that support your main points, making your speech more persuasive and impactful. It gives you the confidence to speak with authority, knowing that you have solid evidence to back up your claims.

To begin your research, start by clearly defining your topic or main message. This will help narrow down your search and ensure that you focus on relevant information. Utilize various sources such as books, online articles, scholarly journals, and reputable websites to gather a wide range of perspectives and data. Remember to evaluate the credibility of your sources and cross-reference information to ensure accuracy.

As you gather information, organize your findings in a systematic and efficient manner. Create an outline or use note-taking techniques that work best for you. Highlight key points and supporting evidence to easily refer back to during your speech preparation. This will not only save you time but also provide a structured framework for your presentation.

In addition to traditional research methods, consider incorporating personal experiences, anecdotes, and stories to add depth and authenticity to your speech. Sharing personal stories not only engages your audience but also helps establish a connection with them, enhancing your self-confidence as a speaker.

Furthermore, do not underestimate the power of visual aids and multimedia in supporting your message. Utilize relevant images, videos, or graphs to complement your speech and make complex information more accessible to your audience. However, always remember to credit your sources and ensure that the visual aids align with your main message.

Lastly, practice incorporating your supporting materials into your speech. Rehearse your delivery, making sure to seamlessly integrate your research while maintaining a natural flow. The more you practice, the more comfortable and confident you will become in presenting your gathered information.

Researching and gathering supporting materials is a fundamental aspect of fearless speaking. By investing time and effort into thorough research, organizing your findings, utilizing personal experiences, and incorporating visual aids, you will not only enhance your content but also boost your self-confidence on any stage. Remember, confidence comes from knowing you have done your due diligence and have the evidence to support your message.

Practicing Techniques for Memorization and Delivery

In the realm of public speaking, one of the most common fears that individuals face is the fear of forgetting their speech or stumbling over their words. However, with the right techniques and strategies, anyone can overcome this fear and become a confident and fearless speaker. This subchapter, titled "Practicing Techniques for Memorization and Delivery," aims to provide valuable insights and guidance on how to develop effective memorization and delivery skills.

For those seeking to enhance their self-confidence and master the art of public speaking, the first step is to establish a solid foundation through diligent practice. Begin by thoroughly understanding your speech or presentation content. Break it down into smaller chunks and memorize each section separately. This technique helps to digest the information more easily and facilitates better retention.

Once you have a clear understanding of the content, it's time to focus on memorization. Explore different methods that work best for you, such as visualization, repetition, or mnemonic devices. Visualizing your speech as a story or associating key points with vivid images can significantly aid in recall. Additionally, practicing your speech out loud and repeating it multiple times will help solidify the words in your memory.

To further enhance the delivery aspect, it is vital to practice in front of a mirror or record yourself speaking. This will help you observe your body language, facial expressions, and overall delivery style. Pay attention to your tone of voice, pacing, and gestures. By reviewing these recordings, you can identify areas for improvement and make necessary adjustments to ensure a confident and engaging delivery.

Another technique to enhance memorization and delivery is to engage in active rehearsal. Instead of simply reading your speech from a script, strive to internalize the content and present it naturally. Practice speaking without relying heavily on notes, allowing yourself to flow with the rhythm of the words. This approach creates a more authentic connection with your audience and boosts your self-confidence.

In conclusion, practicing techniques for memorization and delivery plays a crucial role in developing self-confidence and becoming a fearless speaker. By breaking down the content into manageable sections, employing visualization and repetition, and actively rehearsing, you can overcome the fear of forgetting and deliver your speech with conviction. Remember, practice makes perfect, and with dedication and perseverance, you can embrace confidence on any stage.

Chapter 4: Mastering Non-Verbal Communication

Understanding the Impact of Body Language on Audience Perception

Body language is a powerful form of non-verbal communication that plays a crucial role in how we are perceived by others. Whether we are aware of it or not, our body language can either enhance or undermine our message, especially when it comes to public speaking. In this subchapter, we will explore the profound impact that body language has on audience perception and how it can be harnessed to boost self-confidence on any stage.

When we speak in front of an audience, our body language is constantly being scrutinized. It is said that over 90% of communication is non-verbal, which means that how we hold ourselves, our facial expressions, and our gestures can speak volumes about our confidence and credibility. The way we stand, maintain eye contact, and use our hands can either engage the audience and instill trust or create a disconnect and doubt.

One crucial aspect of body language is posture. Standing tall with an open chest and shoulders back exudes confidence and authority. It shows the audience that you are in control and believe in what you are saying. Conversely, slouching or hunching over can convey insecurity and a lack of conviction, leading to a diminished connection with the audience.

Eye contact is another key element. Making eye contact with individuals in the audience establishes a connection and conveys sincerity. It shows that you value their presence and are actively engaging with them. Avoiding eye contact, on the other hand, can give the impression of disinterest or dishonesty, eroding the audience's trust.

Gestures also play a significant role in body language. Well-placed and purposeful hand movements can enhance the delivery of your message and emphasize key points. However, excessive or distracting gestures can detract from your message and make you appear nervous or unprofessional. Finding a balance and being mindful of your gestures can greatly impact how your audience perceives you.

Understanding how body language influences audience perception is essential for building self-confidence. By consciously harnessing the power of body language, we can project an image of competence, credibility, and authenticity. This, in turn, helps us feel more confident and in control, enabling us to deliver our message with conviction and impact.

In conclusion, body language is a vital tool for effective communication, particularly in public speaking. By understanding the impact of body language on audience perception and learning to control and optimize our non-verbal cues, we can enhance our self-confidence and make a lasting impression on any stage. So, embrace the power of body language and unlock your fearless speaking potential.

Enhancing Gestures, Posture, and Eye Contact

Body language is a powerful tool that can greatly enhance your speaking abilities and boost your self-confidence on any stage. When you learn to express yourself through gestures, maintain proper posture, and establish eye contact with your audience, you not only become a more engaging speaker but also exude confidence and authority. In this subchapter, we will explore the key techniques and tips to help you enhance your gestures, posture, and eye contact, allowing you to become a fearless speaker.

Gestures play a vital role in conveying your message effectively. They can emphasize important points, add clarity, and captivate your audience's attention. By using purposeful and controlled gestures, you can create a visual representation of your words, making them more memorable and impactful. We will discuss various types of gestures, their meanings, and how to incorporate them naturally into your speech.

Maintaining good posture is essential for projecting confidence. When you stand or sit tall with your shoulders back and head held high, you exude an air of self-assurance that captivates your audience. We will delve into the techniques for improving your posture, including exercises and stretches to strengthen your core, which will enhance your overall presence on stage.

Establishing eye contact is crucial for building a connection with your audience. When you look into their eyes, you establish a sense of trust and rapport, making your message more relatable and persuasive. We will explore techniques to help you overcome the fear of eye contact and maintain a natural gaze that engages your listeners.

Additionally, we will address common mistakes to avoid when it comes to gestures, posture, and eye contact. These pitfalls can detract from your message and undermine your self-confidence. By being aware of these potential stumbling blocks, you can steer clear of them and ensure your delivery remains impactful and confident.

Throughout this subchapter, we will provide practical exercises and actionable tips to help you enhance your gestures, posture, and eye contact. By mastering these aspects of body language, you will not only become a fearless speaker but also gain a newfound sense of self-confidence that extends beyond the stage. Whether you are presenting in front of a small group or addressing a large audience, the techniques covered in this subchapter will empower you to embrace confidence and leave a lasting impression on every listener.

Utilizing Vocal Variety and Tone to Convey Confidence

In the realm of public speaking, confidence is the key that unlocks the door to success. It is the catalyst that allows you to connect with your audience and deliver your message with impact. While body language and content play important roles in conveying confidence, your vocal variety and tone are equally crucial. They have the power to captivate your listeners, engage their emotions, and leave a lasting impression.

When it comes to vocal variety, think of your voice as an instrument that can be played in different ways to create a symphony of emotions. Varying your pitch, pace, volume, and emphasis can help you express your ideas more dynamically and keep your audience engaged. Experiment with different vocal techniques during practice to discover what works best for you and your unique speaking style. By doing so, you will bring a sense of authenticity and passion to your delivery.

Tone, on the other hand, refers to the emotional quality of your voice. A confident speaker knows how to infuse their tone with positivity, enthusiasm, and conviction. This helps to build trust and credibility with your audience. Avoid sounding monotone or disinterested, as this can undermine your message and make it difficult for others to connect with you. Instead, strive to convey your passion and belief in what you are saying through your tone. Let your voice resonate with confidence and conviction, and watch as your audience becomes inspired to listen and act upon your words.

It's important to remember that utilizing vocal variety and tone to convey confidence is not about putting on an act or pretending to be someone else. It's about embracing your true self and showcasing the best version of yourself on stage. Authenticity is the key. When you speak from the heart, your vocal variety and tone will naturally reflect your confidence and passion.

So, whether you are addressing a small group of friends or delivering a presentation to a large audience, harness the power of your voice to convey unwavering confidence. Let your vocal variety and tone be the instruments that bring your message to life. Embrace the art of fearless speaking, and watch as your self-confidence soars to new heights. Remember, the world is waiting to hear your voice, so speak up with confidence and make your mark!

Chapter 5: Connecting with Your Audience

Establishing Rapport and Engaging the Crowd

In the realm of public speaking, establishing rapport and engaging the crowd is an essential skill that can make or break your presentation. Whether you're speaking to a small group of colleagues or a large audience of strangers, the ability to connect with your listeners on a personal level is crucial for success. This subchapter will guide you through effective techniques to build rapport and engage your crowd, empowering you to become a fearless and confident speaker.

Rapport is the foundation of any strong connection. It is the mutual understanding, trust, and harmony between the speaker and the audience. To establish rapport, start by acknowledging and respecting your audience's presence. Show genuine interest in them by making eye contact, smiling, and using open body language. This non-verbal communication will help create a positive atmosphere, making your audience more receptive to your message.

Engaging the crowd goes beyond simply capturing their attention; it involves making them an active part of your presentation. Begin by understanding your audience's needs, desires, and interests. Tailor your content accordingly, using relatable stories and examples that resonate with them. Remember, self-confidence comes from knowing your audience and aligning your message with their expectations.

To further engage your crowd, employ interactive techniques such as asking questions, encouraging participation, and utilizing multimedia aids. This will enhance the two-way communication, making your presentation more dynamic and memorable. Additionally, incorporate humor and personal anecdotes to inject authenticity and relatability into your speech. A well-timed joke or a personal story can instantly connect you with your listeners, fostering a sense of camaraderie.

As you speak, be mindful of your tone, pace, and energy. Vary your voice to emphasize key points and maintain a lively rhythm. Use gestures and movement to command the stage and captivate your audience's attention. Remember, self-confidence exudes from commanding your space and projecting enthusiasm.

Lastly, always remain flexible and adaptable during your presentation. Pay attention to the audience's reactions and adapt your approach accordingly. Being aware of their engagement levels allows you to make real-time adjustments, ensuring that you deliver a powerful and impactful speech.

In conclusion, establishing rapport and engaging the crowd are integral to developing self-confidence as a speaker. By connecting with your audience on a personal level, tailoring your content to their needs, employing interactive techniques, and remaining adaptable, you can become a fearless speaker who captivates any crowd. Embrace these techniques, and watch as your self-confidence soars and your speaking skills flourish.

Utilizing Storytelling Techniques to Captivate and Inspire

Storytelling is a powerful tool that has been used for centuries to captivate audiences and inspire change. Whether you are speaking in front of a small group or a large audience, incorporating storytelling techniques into your presentations can help boost your self-confidence and leave a lasting impact on your listeners. In this subchapter, we will explore the art of storytelling and how you can utilize it to become a fearless and confident speaker.

Storytelling has a unique way of engaging our emotions and connecting us on a deeper level. By sharing personal anecdotes, you can create a sense of authenticity and vulnerability that allows your audience to relate to you. These stories humanize you, making you more approachable and relatable, thus boosting your self-confidence as a speaker. Additionally, stories have the power to evoke emotions and inspire action. When you share a story that resonates with your audience, you have the ability to move them to take action or see a situation from a new perspective.

To effectively utilize storytelling techniques, it is important to consider the structure and elements of a compelling story. Begin by setting the stage, introducing the characters and the context of your story. This helps your audience understand the background and become invested in the narrative. Next, build tension and conflict in your story to create anticipation and keep your audience engaged. This can be done by introducing obstacles or challenges that you have faced and overcome. Finally, provide a resolution or a lesson learned, leaving your audience with a sense of inspiration and motivation.

Incorporating storytelling into your presentations not only captivates your audience but also helps to enhance your self-confidence. By sharing personal stories, you are showcasing your vulnerability and authenticity, which can help you build trust with your listeners. Additionally, storytelling allows you to convey your message in a memorable and impactful way, making it more likely that your audience will remember and act upon your words.

In conclusion, storytelling is a powerful tool that can help you become a fearless and confident speaker. By incorporating storytelling techniques into your presentations, you can engage your audience, inspire action, and boost your self-confidence. So, embrace the art of storytelling and discover the transformative power it can bring to your speaking engagements.

Handling Questions and Feedback with Confidence

In the journey towards becoming a fearless speaker, one crucial aspect that cannot be overlooked is the ability to handle questions and feedback with confidence. Whether you are speaking to a small group of colleagues or addressing a large audience, being prepared to handle questions and feedback effectively can greatly enhance your self-confidence and elevate your speaking skills.

First and foremost, it is essential to approach questions and feedback as opportunities for growth rather than as potential threats to your confidence. Understand that questions and feedback are not personal attacks but rather a chance to engage with your audience and provide further clarity or insights. Embracing this mindset will enable you to receive and respond to questions and feedback with a sense of openness and curiosity.

When faced with a question, take a moment to fully understand it before responding. Active listening is key here – listen attentively, repeat or rephrase the question if necessary, and then address it directly. If you are unsure about the answer, be honest and don't hesitate to admit it. Promise to follow up or offer to provide additional information later. This not only demonstrates your humility but also builds trust with your audience.

Handling feedback requires a similar approach. Feedback, whether positive or constructive, should be received graciously and with an open mind. Acknowledge the feedback with gratitude, as it shows that your audience is engaged and invested in your message. Take the time to reflect on the feedback and consider how it aligns with your goals and intentions as a speaker. If the feedback is constructive, use it as an opportunity to learn and grow, making necessary adjustments to improve your future performances.

Confidence in handling questions and feedback also stems from thorough preparation. Anticipate potential questions that may arise from your topic or presentation and prepare thoughtful and concise responses in advance. This preparation will not only enhance your confidence but also enable you to deliver more effective and well-rounded responses.

Lastly, remember that confidence is a skill that can be developed through practice. Seek opportunities to engage in public speaking, attend workshops or join speaking clubs to gain experience in handling questions and feedback. The more you expose yourself to these situations, the more comfortable and confident you will become.

In conclusion, the ability to handle questions and feedback with confidence is a critical aspect of fearless speaking. By embracing questions and feedback as opportunities for growth, actively listening, reflecting on feedback, and preparing in advance, you can develop the self-confidence needed to engage with any audience and deliver impactful speeches. Remember, it is through practice and a growth mindset that you can truly embrace confidence on any stage.

Chapter 6: Managing Nerves and Handling Unexpected Challenges

Implementing Relaxation Techniques to Calm Pre-Speech Anxiety

Introduction:

Pre-speech anxiety is a common experience that many people face when stepping onto a stage or addressing a crowd. The fear of public speaking can be overwhelming, leading to nervousness, sweaty palms, and even a racing heart. However, by implementing relaxation techniques, you can overcome this anxiety and embrace confidence on any stage. In this subchapter, we will explore effective relaxation techniques that can help you calm pre-speech anxiety and boost your self-confidence.

1. Deep Breathing:

One of the simplest and most effective relaxation techniques is deep breathing. It helps to activate the body's relaxation response, reducing stress and anxiety. Before your speech, find a quiet spot, close your eyes, and take slow, deep breaths. Inhale deeply through your nose, hold for a few seconds, and exhale slowly through your mouth. Repeat this process several times, focusing on the sensation of your breath entering and leaving your body. Deep breathing not only calms your mind but also oxygenates your brain, promoting mental clarity and focus.

2. Progressive Muscle Relaxation:

Progressive muscle relaxation is a technique that involves tensing and relaxing specific muscle groups to release tension from the body. Start by tensing the muscles in your toes and then gradually work your way up to your head. As you tense each muscle group, hold the tension for a few seconds, and then release it, allowing the muscles to relax completely. This technique helps to alleviate physical tension and promote a sense of calmness throughout your body.

3. Visualization:
Visualization is a powerful technique that can help you create a mental image of success and boost your confidence. Close your eyes and imagine yourself delivering a successful speech with ease and poise. Visualize the audience responding positively, applauding your words, and connecting with your message. By envisioning success, you are programming your mind to believe in your abilities and reducing anxiety.

4. Affirmations:
Positive affirmations are statements that help to reframe negative thoughts and replace them with empowering beliefs. Before your speech, repeat affirmations such as "I am confident," "I am well-prepared," and "I am a compelling speaker." By affirming positive statements, you are reinforcing self-confidence and reducing anxiety.

Conclusion:
Implementing relaxation techniques can significantly calm pre-speech anxiety and enhance your self-confidence. Deep breathing, progressive muscle relaxation, visualization, and affirmations are powerful tools to help you overcome fear and embrace confidence on any stage. Remember, practice is key. The more you incorporate these techniques into your daily routine, the more natural they will become. By mastering relaxation techniques, you will be well-equipped to

conquer your fear of public speaking and become a fearless and confident speaker.

Dealing with Technical Difficulties and Unexpected Interruptions

In the world of public speaking, technical difficulties and unexpected interruptions can be nerve-wracking and throw even the most confident speakers off balance. However, it is important to remember that these challenges are a normal part of the speaking experience. By being prepared and flexible, you can overcome these obstacles and continue to deliver a powerful and fearless presentation.

First and foremost, it is crucial to always have a backup plan. Technical difficulties can range from malfunctioning projectors to audio issues. Carry a USB drive with your presentation saved in multiple formats, such as PowerPoint and PDF, to ensure compatibility with different equipment. Additionally, consider having a printed copy of your speech or presentation on hand as a last resort. By having these backups, you can easily adapt to any technical glitch that arises.

Moreover, practice improvisation skills. Unexpected interruptions, such as a fire alarm or a sudden power outage, can completely disrupt your flow. In these situations, it is important to stay calm and think quickly. Take a deep breath, assess the situation, and decide the best course of action. If there is an interruption that cannot be ignored, consider using humor to lighten the mood and engage your audience. This demonstrates your ability to think on your feet and adapt to unforeseen circumstances, further boosting your self-confidence.

It is also beneficial to establish a connection with your audience. Building rapport and establishing a positive relationship can help alleviate tension during technical difficulties or interruptions. Engage with your audience through eye contact, genuine smiles, and open body language. By creating a friendly and welcoming environment, your audience will be more understanding and supportive when challenges arise.

Finally, maintain a positive mindset. Remember that technical difficulties and unexpected interruptions happen to even the most experienced speakers. Instead of viewing them as obstacles, see them as opportunities to demonstrate your resilience and adaptability. Embrace the unexpected as a chance to connect with your audience on a deeper level and show them your authentic self.

In conclusion, technical difficulties and unexpected interruptions are realities that every speaker may face. By being prepared, practicing improvisation skills, building rapport with your audience, and maintaining a positive mindset, you can navigate these challenges with confidence and continue to deliver fearless and impactful presentations. Remember, it is not about the obstacles you encounter, but how you overcome them that truly defines your speaking prowess.

Turning Mistakes into Opportunities for Growth

Mistakes are inevitable. They are a natural part of life, and they happen to everyone. However, it is not the mistakes themselves that define us, but how we choose to respond to them. In the realm of self-confidence, the ability to turn mistakes into opportunities for growth can be a powerful tool for personal development and success.

When it comes to public speaking, mistakes can feel particularly daunting. The fear of making errors, forgetting lines, or stumbling over words can be paralyzing. However, it is important to remember that mistakes are not the end of the world. In fact, they can often be the catalyst for growth and improvement.

One way to transform mistakes into opportunities for growth is by reframing them as learning experiences. Instead of dwelling on the embarrassment or disappointment of making a mistake, shift your perspective and view it as a chance to learn and improve. Reflect on what went wrong and identify areas where you can make adjustments for future presentations. By embracing mistakes as valuable lessons, you can develop a mindset of continuous improvement and resilience.

Another powerful strategy is to practice self-compassion. It is easy to be harsh on ourselves when we make mistakes, especially in the realm of self-confidence. However, beating yourself up over a mistake will only hinder your progress. Instead, treat yourself with kindness and understanding. Recognize that mistakes are a part of the learning process and that everyone makes them. By practicing self-compassion, you can bounce back from mistakes more quickly and confidently.

Furthermore, mistakes can provide an opportunity to connect with your audience on a deeper level. Authenticity is a key component of effective public speaking, and admitting and addressing mistakes openly can help you build trust and rapport with your listeners. By demonstrating vulnerability and humility, you can create a genuine connection that resonates with your audience.

In conclusion, turning mistakes into opportunities for growth is a crucial skill for building self-confidence. By reframing mistakes as learning experiences, practicing self-compassion, and using them as a platform for connection, you can transform setbacks into stepping stones towards personal and professional growth. Embrace your mistakes, learn from them, and let them propel you to new heights of confidence on any stage. Remember, it is not the absence of mistakes that defines your journey but rather how you overcome and grow from them.

Chapter 7: Enhancing Your Presentation Skills

Utilizing Visual Aids Effectively to Enhance Communication

In today's fast-paced world, effective communication is crucial for success in various aspects of life. Whether you are giving a presentation at work, speaking at a conference, or even engaging in a casual conversation, being able to convey your thoughts and ideas clearly is essential. One powerful tool that can greatly enhance your communication skills is the effective use of visual aids.

Visual aids are any visual elements or tools that help support and reinforce your message. They can range from simple props, charts, and graphs, to more complex multimedia presentations. By incorporating visual aids into your communication, you not only capture your audience's attention but also facilitate better understanding and retention of information.

One of the key benefits of using visual aids is that they cater to different learning styles. While some individuals are auditory learners who absorb information through listening, others are visual learners who grasp concepts better through visual representations. By incorporating visual aids, you ensure that you are catering to both types of learners, allowing them to better comprehend and engage with your message.

Moreover, visual aids act as a powerful memory aid. Research shows that people remember information better when it is presented in a visual format. By utilizing visual aids effectively, you can make your message more memorable and leave a lasting impact on your audience.

When using visual aids, it is important to keep a few key principles in mind. Firstly, simplicity is key. Avoid cluttering your visuals with excessive text or complex graphics. Instead, focus on conveying your main points concisely and clearly. Use bullet points, diagrams, and visuals that are easy to understand and support your message effectively.

Secondly, ensure that your visual aids are visually appealing. Use colors, fonts, and layouts that are visually attractive and aid in conveying your message. Remember that visuals should enhance your communication, not distract from it.

Lastly, practice using your visual aids before your actual presentation. Familiarize yourself with the content, timing, and transitions to ensure a smooth delivery. This will help build your confidence and allow you to engage with your audience more effectively.

In conclusion, utilizing visual aids effectively is a powerful way to enhance your communication skills and boost self-confidence. By catering to different learning styles, aiding memory retention, and delivering information concisely, visual aids can make your message more impactful and memorable. So, embrace the power of visual aids and unlock your potential as a fearless speaker.

Incorporating Humor and Engaging Techniques to Connect with the Audience

Laughter is a universal language that has the power to break down barriers and create connections. Incorporating humor and engaging techniques into your public speaking can not only captivate your audience but also boost your self-confidence on any stage. In this subchapter, we will explore the art of infusing humor and engaging techniques into your presentations, helping you become a fearless speaker who connects with everyone.

Humor is a fantastic tool to engage your audience and make your message memorable. By incorporating well-timed jokes, funny anecdotes, or humorous visuals, you can instantly capture your audience's attention and create a relaxed atmosphere. However, it is crucial to use humor appropriately and tastefully, considering the cultural background and sensitivities of your audience. Remember, the goal is to entertain, not offend.

Engaging techniques go beyond humor and involve various strategies to make your presentation interactive and captivating. One effective technique is storytelling. By sharing personal stories or narratives that relate to your topic, you can create an emotional connection with your audience. People love stories, and incorporating them into your speech helps to make your message relatable and memorable.

Another engaging technique is audience participation. Encourage your audience to participate actively, whether through raising hands, responding to questions, or even playing interactive games. By involving your listeners, you create a sense of involvement and make them feel like an integral part of the presentation. This interaction not only keeps their attention but also boosts their confidence and involvement in the discussion.

Visual aids are also powerful tools to engage your audience. Using captivating visuals, such as images, videos, or infographics, can enhance your message and provide a break from constant verbal communication. Visuals help to stimulate interest, reinforce key points, and create a dynamic and visually appealing presentation.

Lastly, incorporating humor and engaging techniques requires practice and preparation. Experiment with different humorous elements, engaging techniques, and visual aids during your rehearsals. Take note of what works and what doesn't, and be open to adjusting your approach based on audience reactions.

In conclusion, incorporating humor and engaging techniques into your public speaking can significantly impact your self-confidence and connect with your audience. Utilize humor tastefully, incorporate storytelling, encourage audience participation, use captivating visuals, and practice diligently to become a fearless speaker who leaves a lasting impression on every individual in the room.

Creating Memorable Endings and Calls to Action

The Art of Fearless Speaking: Embrace Confidence on Any Stage

Chapter 7: Creating Memorable Endings and Calls to Action

In the world of public speaking, the ending is just as important as the beginning. It is the lasting impression you leave on your audience, the final words that resonate in their minds long after your speech is over. In this chapter, we will explore the art of creating memorable endings and crafting powerful calls to action, ensuring that your message stays with your audience and inspires them to take action.

To effectively create a memorable ending, it is crucial to summarize your key points and reiterate your main message. Remind your audience of the journey you took them on and the insights they gained along the way. This recap not only reinforces your main ideas but also helps the audience remember and connect with your speech on a deeper level.

However, a memorable ending goes beyond just summarizing. It should evoke emotion and leave a lasting impact. Consider incorporating a personal story or anecdote that relates to your message, or share a powerful quote that encapsulates the essence of your speech. By tapping into the emotions of your audience, you create an ending that resonates with them on a personal level.

In addition to creating memorable endings, it is essential to include a strong call to action. A call to action is a clear and concise statement that tells your audience what you want them to do after hearing your speech. Whether it is encouraging them to take a specific action, adopt a new mindset, or make a change in their lives, a well-crafted call to action can inspire your audience to take the next step.

To ensure your call to action is effective, make it specific, actionable, and realistic. Clearly outline the steps your audience can take to achieve the desired outcome. Use persuasive language to motivate and engage them, and offer support or resources to help them along the way. By providing a roadmap for action, you empower your audience to translate the inspiration they feel into tangible results.

In conclusion, creating memorable endings and crafting powerful calls to action are essential skills in the art of fearless speaking. By summarizing your main points, tapping into emotions, and providing a clear call to action, you leave a lasting impression on your audience and inspire them to take action. Remember, the ending is your final opportunity to connect with your audience and make a lasting impact, so make it count.

This chapter is dedicated to helping you master the art of creating memorable endings and calls to action, ensuring that your speeches leave a lasting impression on every individual in your audience. By embracing the techniques and strategies outlined in this chapter, you will develop the self-confidence to captivate any audience and inspire them to take action.

Chapter 8: Embracing Feedback and Continuous Improvement

Seeking Constructive Criticism to Enhance Performance

Receiving feedback can be a daunting experience for many individuals, especially when it comes to public speaking. However, if you truly desire to boost your self-confidence and become a fearless speaker, seeking constructive criticism is an essential step on your journey.

Constructive criticism serves as a valuable tool for self-improvement. It provides you with an opportunity to identify areas of growth, refine your skills, and enhance your overall performance. While it may initially feel uncomfortable, embracing feedback is crucial for personal development and building unwavering self-confidence.

One of the key benefits of seeking constructive criticism is gaining an outside perspective. When we are on stage, it is easy to become blind to our own shortcomings. Having someone offer an objective viewpoint can help us identify areas for improvement that we may have otherwise overlooked. It allows us to see our speaking skills from a fresh angle and make the necessary adjustments to enhance our performance.

Moreover, constructive criticism helps us identify patterns and tendencies that may hinder our self-confidence. By receiving feedback from others, we can become aware of any nervous habits or negative thought patterns that may be holding us back. Armed with this knowledge, we can then address these issues and work towards overcoming them, ultimately boosting our self-confidence on stage.

It is important to approach constructive criticism with an open mind and a growth mindset. Rather than viewing it as a personal attack, see it as an opportunity for growth. Remember that the goal is not perfection but continuous improvement. Embrace the feedback you receive, and be open to making adjustments that will ultimately enhance your speaking abilities.

To seek constructive criticism effectively, surround yourself with a supportive network of individuals who genuinely want to see you succeed. Seek out mentors, coaches, or fellow speakers who can provide valuable insights and guidance. Engage in conversations with your audience, asking for their feedback and suggestions. By actively seeking out constructive criticism, you will not only improve your speaking skills but also build a network of supportive individuals who share your passion for self-confidence and personal growth.

In conclusion, seeking constructive criticism is an essential step in enhancing your performance and building self-confidence as a speaker. Embrace feedback as a valuable tool for growth, be open to making adjustments, and surround yourself with a supportive network. By doing so, you will undoubtedly become a fearless speaker who captivates any audience with ease.

Developing a Personalized Feedback and Improvement Plan

In the journey of becoming a fearless speaker, it is crucial to understand that self-confidence is not an inherent trait possessed by a lucky few. It is a skill that can be developed and honed over time. One of the most effective ways to boost your self-confidence in public speaking is by creating a personalized feedback and improvement plan.

Feedback is a powerful tool that allows us to identify our strengths and weaknesses. By seeking feedback from others, we gain valuable insights into how we are perceived as speakers. This feedback can be obtained from trusted friends, family members, or even professional speech coaches. It is important to choose individuals who will provide constructive criticism and support your growth.

Once you have gathered feedback, it is time to analyze it and create an improvement plan tailored to your needs. Start by identifying the areas where you excel and celebrate those achievements. This will boost your confidence and remind you of your capabilities as a speaker.

Next, focus on the areas that require improvement. Break down these areas into smaller, manageable goals. For example, if you struggle with maintaining eye contact, set a goal to practice making eye contact with one person in every conversation you have. By setting specific and achievable goals, you create a pathway to success.

In addition to setting goals, it is important to develop a practice routine that incorporates targeted exercises to address your weaknesses. For example, if you struggle with projecting your voice, practice speaking loudly and clearly in front of a mirror or record yourself and listen for areas that need improvement. Consistency is key in developing any skill, so make sure to allocate dedicated time for practice in your daily routine.

Another crucial aspect of your feedback and improvement plan is accountability. Share your goals and progress with a trusted friend or mentor who can provide support and hold you accountable. Regular check-ins will help you stay motivated and on track.

Remember, developing self-confidence in public speaking is a journey that requires patience and perseverance. Embrace the process of self-improvement and be open to continuous feedback. With a personalized feedback and improvement plan, you will gradually overcome your insecurities and become a fearless speaker who captivates any audience.

Embracing a Growth Mindset for Ongoing Success

In the journey towards self-confidence, one of the most powerful tools we can utilize is the mindset we bring to the table. A growth mindset, when embraced wholeheartedly, has the potential to transform our lives and propel us towards ongoing success. In this subchapter, we will explore the concept of a growth mindset and how it can be applied to our quest for fearless speaking and self-confidence.

A growth mindset is the belief that our abilities and intelligence can be developed through dedication, effort, and a willingness to learn. It is the understanding that our skills and talents are not fixed, but rather can be improved upon with practice and perseverance. By adopting this mindset, we free ourselves from the limitations of a fixed mindset that tells us we are either born with certain abilities or not.

When it comes to speaking confidently on any stage, embracing a growth mindset is crucial. It allows us to see setbacks and failures as opportunities for growth rather than indicators of our worth. Instead of shying away from challenges, we welcome them as chances to learn and improve. By viewing public speaking as a skill that can be developed, we take the pressure off ourselves to be perfect from the start and instead focus on progress.

Cultivating a growth mindset involves nurturing a love for learning and embracing the process of improvement. It means being open to feedback and constructive criticism, seeing it as a valuable tool for growth rather than a personal attack. It also involves reframing our self-talk, replacing negative thoughts with positive affirmations that reinforce our belief in our ability to grow and succeed.

By embracing a growth mindset, we not only enhance our self-confidence in public speaking but in all areas of our lives. We become more resilient, adaptable, and willing to take on challenges that push us out of our comfort zones. We understand that failure is not the end, but a stepping stone towards success.

In conclusion, a growth mindset is a powerful tool for ongoing success and self-confidence. By adopting this mindset, we unlock our true potential and become unstoppable in our pursuit of fearless speaking. So, let us embrace the growth mindset, nurture our love for learning, and watch as our self-confidence soars to new heights.

Chapter 9: Overcoming Fear of Specific Speaking Situations

Speaking in Small Group Settings or Meetings

In today's fast-paced world, the ability to communicate effectively in small group settings or meetings is crucial for personal and professional success. Whether you are participating in a team project, attending a business meeting, or engaging in a social gathering, your ability to speak confidently and assertively can greatly impact the outcomes and the impression you leave on others.

Small group settings or meetings can sometimes be intimidating, especially if you struggle with self-confidence. However, by embracing a few key strategies, you can overcome your fears and become a fearless speaker in any setting.

First and foremost, it is important to prepare yourself before the meeting or gathering. Take the time to understand the purpose and goals of the meeting, as well as the topics that will be discussed. This will allow you to gather your thoughts and formulate relevant points to contribute. Additionally, practicing what you want to say beforehand can help boost your confidence and reduce anxiety.

When it comes to speaking in small group settings, it is crucial to actively listen and engage with others. Pay attention to what others are saying, and be prepared to respond or build upon their ideas. This not only demonstrates respect and interest in others' opinions, but it also allows you to establish yourself as an active participant in the discussion.

One of the keys to speaking confidently in small group settings is to be concise and clear with your words. Avoid rambling or going off on tangents. Instead, focus on delivering your message in a succinct and impactful manner. This will ensure that your ideas are easily understood and remembered by others.

Furthermore, it is important to be aware of your body language and non-verbal cues. Maintain eye contact with others, use gestures to emphasize your points, and adopt an open and receptive posture. These non-verbal signals can convey confidence and establish a connection with your audience.

Lastly, remember that confidence is not about being perfect or knowing everything. It is about embracing your unique perspective and being willing to contribute to the conversation. Do not be afraid to ask questions or seek clarification if needed. This shows that you are engaged and committed to the discussion.

By implementing these strategies, you can become a fearless speaker in small group settings or meetings. Remember, self-confidence is a skill that can be developed through practice and experience. So, embrace the opportunity to speak up and share your ideas. Your voice matters, and by speaking with confidence, you can make a lasting impact in any small group setting.

Presenting to Large Audiences or Conferences

Speaking in front of a large audience or at a conference can be an intimidating experience for many people. The thought of addressing a room full of strangers can trigger feelings of anxiety and self-doubt. However, with the right mindset and preparation, you can learn to embrace confidence and deliver a powerful presentation that leaves a lasting impact.

The first step in presenting to large audiences or conferences is to cultivate self-confidence. Believe in yourself and your abilities as a speaker. Remind yourself that you have valuable insights to share and that your audience is eager to hear from you. Visualize success and focus on positive outcomes rather than dwelling on potential mistakes.

Preparation is key when it comes to presenting to large audiences. Research your topic thoroughly and organize your thoughts in a logical manner. Create a clear and concise outline that will guide you through your presentation. Practice your delivery, paying attention to your body language and vocal tone. Rehearse in front of a mirror or record yourself to identify areas for improvement.

Engaging your audience is crucial in keeping their attention throughout your presentation. Use storytelling techniques to make your content relatable and memorable. Incorporate visuals such as slides or props to enhance understanding and retention. Encourage audience participation through questions or interactive activities. Remember, the more engaged your audience is, the more impactful your message will be.

Managing nerves is another important aspect of presenting to large audiences. Before stepping on stage, use relaxation techniques such as deep breathing or visualization to calm your mind and body. Remind yourself of your preparation and positive affirmations. Embrace the adrenaline rush as a sign of excitement rather than fear. Channel that energy into your presentation, allowing it to fuel your passion and enthusiasm.

During your presentation, maintain a confident and poised demeanor. Stand tall, make eye contact, and speak clearly and audibly. Use gestures and body language to emphasize key points. Pace yourself, allowing pauses for emphasis and to give your audience time to absorb information. Remember to smile and project enthusiasm, as your energy will be contagious.

In conclusion, presenting to large audiences or conferences requires self-confidence, preparation, engagement, and effective communication skills. By embracing these principles and incorporating them into your presentations, you can captivate your audience and deliver a fearless and impactful performance. Remember, every great speaker was once a beginner, so embrace the challenge and seize every opportunity to grow and excel in your public speaking journey.

Overcoming Fear of Public Speaking Online or through Video Conferencing

In today's digital age, public speaking has taken on a new form with the rise of online platforms and video conferencing. While this may seem like a relief for those who fear speaking in front of a live audience, it can still be a daunting task. The fear of public speaking is a common one, but with the right mindset and strategies, it is possible to overcome it and embrace confidence on any stage, even if that stage is virtual.

One of the first steps to overcoming the fear of public speaking online is to recognize that the same principles apply, regardless of the platform. The key is to focus on your message and connect with your audience, just as you would in a traditional setting. Remember that the medium may have changed, but the fundamentals of effective communication remain the same.

To build self-confidence in online or video conferencing speaking, it is essential to practice and prepare. Take advantage of the technology available to you by recording yourself and watching the playback. This will help you identify areas for improvement and gain familiarity with your own speaking style. Additionally, rehearse your presentation multiple times to build confidence in your content and delivery.

Another important aspect of overcoming fear in this context is to embrace the virtual environment. Understand that you have the ability to control your surroundings and set up a space that is comfortable and conducive to speaking confidently. Pay attention to lighting, background, and audio quality to ensure that your audience can fully engage with your message.

Furthermore, it is crucial to engage with your audience through this virtual medium. Utilize interactive features such as polls, chat functions, or question-and-answer sessions to encourage participation and create a sense of connection. Remember that public speaking is not a one-sided conversation; it is an opportunity to engage, inspire, and educate.

Finally, seek support and feedback from others. Join online communities or forums where you can connect with fellow speakers and gain insights from their experiences. Consider enrolling in public speaking courses or workshops specifically tailored for online or video conferencing platforms. Surrounding yourself with a supportive network can help boost your confidence and provide valuable guidance as you navigate this new speaking landscape.

In conclusion, overcoming the fear of public speaking online or through video conferencing requires a combination of mindset, practice, and embracing the virtual environment. By focusing on your message, preparing thoroughly, engaging with your audience, and seeking support, you can overcome your fear and confidently deliver impactful presentations in any setting. Remember, the stage may have changed, but your ability to inspire and influence others remains steadfast.

Chapter 10: Maintaining Fearless Speaking in Everyday Life

Applying Public Speaking Techniques in Professional Settings

Public speaking is an essential skill in today's professional world. Whether you are presenting to a group of colleagues, pitching a business proposal, or leading a team meeting, the ability to effectively communicate your ideas is crucial. In this subchapter, we will explore how to apply public speaking techniques in various professional settings, helping you embrace self-confidence and excel in your career.

One of the first steps to becoming a fearless speaker in professional settings is to understand your audience. Consider their knowledge, interests, and expectations. Tailor your content to meet their needs and engage them from the start. Begin with a strong opening that grabs their attention and clearly states the purpose of your presentation. Use storytelling techniques to connect with your audience emotionally and make your message memorable.

Another key aspect of professional public speaking is mastering your body language and delivery. Maintain good posture, make eye contact, and use gestures to emphasize important points. Practice your speech to ensure a confident and natural delivery. Pay attention to your tone of voice, volume, and pace, adjusting them to suit the setting and the message you want to convey.

Visual aids can be powerful tools in professional presentations. Use slides, graphs, and charts to support your key points and provide visual representation of your data. However, be cautious not to overload your slides with text or information. Keep them simple, visually appealing, and easy to comprehend at a glance.

In professional settings, it is essential to handle questions and feedback effectively. Anticipate potential questions and prepare concise and thoughtful answers. Be open to feedback and actively listen to others' perspectives. Respond respectfully and constructively, acknowledging different viewpoints. This will demonstrate your professionalism and ability to work collaboratively.

To further enhance your public speaking skills, consider seeking opportunities for professional development. Attend workshops, join Toastmasters clubs, or engage in public speaking courses. Practice regularly, both in formal and informal settings, to build your confidence and refine your delivery.

Remember, self-confidence is key in professional public speaking. Believe in yourself and your abilities. Embrace the opportunity to share your knowledge and ideas. With practice and dedication, you can become a fearless speaker, making a lasting impact in your professional life.

In conclusion, applying public speaking techniques in professional settings is a valuable skill that can boost your self-confidence and advance your career. By understanding your audience, mastering body language and delivery, utilizing visual aids effectively, and handling questions and feedback with professionalism, you can become a confident and persuasive speaker. Through continuous practice and a belief in yourself, you can embrace the art of fearless speaking and excel in any professional setting.

Utilizing Fearless Speaking Skills in Personal Relationships and Social Settings

In our everyday lives, personal relationships and social settings play a crucial role in our overall happiness and well-being. Whether it is expressing our thoughts and feelings to loved ones or engaging in conversations with acquaintances and strangers, effective communication is key. However, for many individuals, the fear of speaking up and being heard can be a significant obstacle in building self-confidence and forming meaningful connections.

"The Art of Fearless Speaking: Embrace Confidence on Any Stage" provides invaluable insights and practical strategies to overcome this fear and utilize fearless speaking skills in personal relationships and social settings. This subchapter is designed to empower every individual, regardless of their background or experience, with the tools to communicate effectively and confidently.

One of the fundamental aspects emphasized in this subchapter is the importance of self-confidence. Self-confidence is the foundation upon which successful communication is built. By understanding and embracing our own unique qualities and strengths, we can project a sense of assurance and authenticity in our interactions. The book explores various techniques and exercises to help individuals develop and maintain their self-confidence, empowering them to express themselves freely and fearlessly.

Moreover, this subchapter delves into the art of active listening. Effective communication is a two-way street, and listening attentively is just as important as speaking. By honing our listening skills, we can demonstrate genuine interest, empathy, and understanding in our personal relationships and social interactions. This subchapter provides insights and strategies for becoming an active listener, fostering stronger connections and establishing trust with those around us.

In addition to self-confidence and active listening, the subchapter also delves into techniques for managing and overcoming communication anxiety. Fear of judgment, rejection, or embarrassment often hinders our ability to express ourselves openly. With practical exercises and mindset shifts, this subchapter aims to help individuals conquer their fears and communicate fearlessly, thereby enhancing their personal relationships and social interactions.

"The Art of Fearless Speaking: Embrace Confidence on Any Stage" provides a comprehensive guide for individuals seeking to improve their self-confidence and communication skills in personal relationships and social settings. By embracing fearless speaking techniques, readers will learn to express themselves authentically, connect deeply with others, and navigate social situations with ease and grace. This subchapter is a valuable resource for anyone looking to enhance their self-confidence and make a lasting impact in their personal and social lives.

Embracing Fearless Communication in Advocacy and Leadership Roles

In today's fast-paced and interconnected world, effective communication skills have become more critical than ever, especially in advocacy and leadership roles. Whether you are a seasoned public speaker or someone struggling with self-confidence, fear and anxiety can often hinder your ability to express yourself with conviction and clarity. However, by embracing fearless communication techniques, you can unlock your true potential and become a powerful advocate and leader.

Fearless communication is not about eliminating fear altogether, but rather about acknowledging and channeling it in a positive way. It is about recognizing that fear is a natural response to the unknown and using it as a catalyst for personal growth and development. By embracing your fears and stepping outside your comfort zone, you can build self-confidence and become a more effective advocate and leader.

One of the first steps toward embracing fearless communication is understanding the power of vulnerability. It is essential to recognize that vulnerability is not a weakness but a strength. By being open and authentic, you can connect with your audience on a deeper level, making your message more relatable and impactful. Embracing vulnerability allows you to share your stories and experiences genuinely, inspiring others to do the same.

Another key aspect of fearless communication is mastering the art of active listening. Effective advocacy and leadership require empathy and understanding, and this can only be achieved by truly listening to your audience. By actively engaging with others, you can create a safe and inclusive environment where everyone's voice is heard and respected. This fosters trust and collaboration, making you a more influential advocate and leader.

Furthermore, embracing fearless communication involves developing strong storytelling skills. Humans are naturally drawn to stories, and they have the power to evoke emotions and inspire action. By crafting compelling narratives that resonate with your audience, you can effectively convey your message and motivate others to take action. Storytelling allows you to connect with people on an emotional level, making your advocacy and leadership efforts much more impactful.

In a world that often values perfection and conformity, embracing fearless communication is a revolutionary act. It requires embracing your fears, being vulnerable, and actively listening to others. It demands that you step into your power and share your unique voice with the world. By doing so, you can inspire confidence in yourself and others, becoming an influential advocate and leader in your chosen field. So, embrace fearless communication, unlock your true potential, and make a lasting impact on the world.

Conclusion: Embrace Confidence on Any Stage

In today's fast-paced world, self-confidence is a skill that can truly set you apart from the crowd. Whether you are a student, a professional, an entrepreneur, or simply someone looking to improve their personal growth, developing self-confidence is essential to achieving your goals and living a fulfilled life.

"The Art of Fearless Speaking: Embrace Confidence on Any Stage" is a comprehensive guide that has taken you through a journey of self-discovery, empowering you to overcome your fears and step onto any stage with confidence. Throughout this book, we have explored various strategies, techniques, and mindsets that will help you embrace your true potential and become a fearless speaker.

Understanding that confidence is not something we are born with, but rather a skill that can be developed and mastered, is the first step towards unleashing your inner confidence. We have debunked the myth that confident individuals are born that way, emphasizing that confidence is a result of practice, self-awareness, and continuous growth.

We have explored the power of positive self-talk, affirmations, and visualization techniques as tools to reprogram our mindset and cultivate a deep sense of self-confidence. By replacing self-doubt with positive thoughts and beliefs, you can transform your inner critic into your biggest cheerleader.

Furthermore, we have delved into the importance of preparation, body language, and vocal delivery in conveying confidence to your audience. From mastering the art of storytelling to effectively using visual aids, every aspect of public speaking has been covered to ensure that you not only feel confident but also captivate your listeners.

In the journey towards embracing confidence on any stage, we have also addressed the fear of judgment and rejection. By understanding that everyone has their own insecurities and that criticism is merely a reflection of others' perspectives, you can liberate yourself from the fear of what others may think, allowing your authentic self to shine.

Remember, confidence is not about being flawless; it is about embracing your imperfections and embracing them as part of your unique journey. Every stumble and setback is an opportunity to learn and grow. By continuously challenging yourself and pushing beyond your comfort zone, you will witness your confidence soar to new heights.

As we conclude this chapter, I encourage you to continue practicing the techniques and strategies shared in this book. Embrace every stage in your life with confidence, whether it's delivering a presentation, engaging in a conversation, or pursuing your dreams. Remember that self-confidence is not limited to public speaking; it is a skill that will positively impact every aspect of your life.

So, go forth and fearlessly embrace confidence on any stage. You have the power within you to become the best version of yourself. Believe in yourself, trust your abilities, and let your confidence shine through. The world is waiting for you to make your mark.

www.ingramcontent.com/pod-product-compliance
Lightning Source LLC
LaVergne TN
LVHW052003060526
838201LV00059B/3820